SPOTLIGHT ON SOCIAL AND EMOTIONAL LEARNING

IN CHARGE AND UNSTOPPABLE

DEVELOPING ORGANIZATIONAL SKILLS

JILL KEPPELER

PowerKiDS press™

NEW YORK

Published in 2020 by The Rosen Publishing Group, Inc.
29 East 21st Street, New York, NY 10010

Editor: Elizabeth Krajnik
Designer: Michael Flynn

Photo Credits: Cover kate_sept2004/E+/Getty Images; cover, pp. 1, 3–4, 6, 8, 10–14, 16–20, 22–24 (background) TairA/Shutterstock.com; p. 5 (main) Westend61/Getty Images; p. 5 (inset) Veja/Shutterstock.com; p. 7 Reggie Casagrande/Photolibrary/Getty Images; p. 9 Vincenzo Lombardo/Getty Images Entertainment/Getty Images; p. 10 Monkey Business Images/Shutterstock.com; p. 11 Charles Ommanney/Getty Images News/Getty Images; p. 12 Syda Productions/Shutterstock.com; p. 13 Photographee.eu/Shutterstock.com; p. 15 Niall Carson/PA Images/Getty Images; p. 16 Slavoljub Pantelic/Shutterstock.com; p. 17 Leszek Glasner/Shutterstock.com; p. 18 Littlekidmoment/Shutterstock.com; p. 19 Savicic/Shutterstock.com; p. 21 Africa Studio/Shutterstock.com; p. 22 Dima Sidelnikov/Shutterstock.com.

Cataloging-in-Publication Data

Names: Keppeler, Jill.
Title: In charge and unstoppable: developing organizational skills / Jill Keppeler.
Description: New York : PowerKids Press, 2020. | Series: Spotlight on social and emotional learning | Includes glossary and index.
Identifiers: ISBN 9781725302044 (pbk.) | ISBN 9781725302235 (library bound) | ISBN 9781725302143 (6pack)
Subjects: LCSH: Time management--Juvenile literature. | Organization--Juvenile literature.
Classification: LCC HD69.T54 K47 2020 | DDC 646.700835'2--dc23

Manufactured in the United States of America

CPSIA Compliance Information: Batch #CSPK19. For further information contact Rosen Publishing, New York, New York at 1-800-237-9932.

CONTENTS

CHAPTER ONE

SO MANY THINGS

Even though you're young, you probably have a lot of things going on in your life. You have school and homework. You may have **chores** and duties you do to help your parents around your home. You might have sports practices or music lessons or other things you do for fun. Even if these things are fun, though, you still need to find time for them.

To get everything done, it's important to be organized. You need to know where your schoolbooks, **assignments**, and sports and hobby **equipment** are and make sure you're ready for your activities. You might find this easy—or you might find it to be really hard! Maybe you sometimes feel like everything is out of control. But you can take charge and get organized—you just need to take things one step at a time.

Kids today can have lots to do! Good organizational skills can help make it easier to stay on top of everything.

CHAPTER TWO

WHY BE ORGANIZED?

Organization can help keep you from being **overwhelmed** with things you have to do and give you more time for fun things. Imagine this: You have to do your math homework after school and then practice your violin before you can play video games with your friends. But what if you can't find your assignment? Maybe you wrote it down on a little piece of paper—somewhere.

You dig through your backpack and spend a long time looking for it before you find it crumpled up at the bottom. And then, where's your math book? Do you have a sharpened pencil to work with and a good eraser? And then, what happened to your violin? Is it in your room? Did you leave it at school? Being organized—knowing where all these things are and being ready to go—will help you avoid wasting time.

Do you lose things a lot? It can be annoying and waste a lot of time. If you lose your homework, your teacher might give you a zero.

CHAPTER THREE

IT'S A SKILL

Some people seem naturally organized. They're always ready and they always seem to know where everything is. Even if this doesn't come naturally to you, though, you can learn organizational skills. You can practice them just like you practice sports or music. With practice, you'll get better at them. One important place to start is to figure out your **priorities**. What do you need to do? Those things come first. Then, what do you *want* to do?

Sometimes it helps people to make lists of what they need to do and what they want to do. Then you can check off one "need-to-do" thing at a time until you get to "want-to-do" things. You can also use lists to keep track of your **extracurricular** activities such as sports practices or music lessons.

Even famous people use lists! Businessman and billionaire Richard Branson, pictured here, has written about how he uses to-do lists to help get things done.

CHAPTER FOUR

BREAK IT DOWN

Breaking things you need to do down into smaller pieces can help you stay organized and keep you from being overwhelmed. First, get ready to do a task. This means getting together everything you need (for homework, this could mean assignments, pencils, books, and paper) and going to the place where you need to do the task. This includes making sure you know where to get all the things you need, such as having your assignments all written down neatly.

Former First Lady Michelle Obama has spoken about the importance of organization. In November 2016, she said about being a mother, "You have to be **fiercely** organized to get anything done."

Next, you need to **focus** on the task and do it. It sounds easy, but this can be the hardest part! You have to learn to deal with **distractions**. Last, you need to finish the task and make sure everything's organized. It doesn't matter if you did your homework if you forget to take it into school the next day.

CHAPTER FIVE

WRITE IT DOWN

For the first step, sometimes you need to think ahead. It's too late to figure out that you need a book for a school project when you're already home, the project is due the next day, and the book is at school. This is why it can be valuable to write things down and keep an assignment notebook. You can write down all the **information** about your school assignments in your assignment notebook and check it before you leave school each day.

Writing things down is a great way to help you remember them!

Once you're home and ready to work on the task, get all the things you need together and go to the place where you'll do the work. It can be very helpful to have a workplace in a quiet area where you can be alone. If not, try to find another place where you can work in peace.

CHAPTER SIX

DON'T PUT IT OFF!

It can be tempting to procrastinate when you have something that you don't want to do. Procrastination means that you're slow about doing a task and put it off until a later time. This is understandable, but it can lead to more disorganization. You may have to rush to get the task done on time and put off other tasks. This can start a chain of procrastination and it doesn't help you stay organized!

Even though procrastination is tempting, try not to do it too much. If you catch yourself saying "I'll just do it tomorrow," try thinking about what it will be like doing it tomorrow and how much busier that might make the next day. Or, take a small step and just start the task. Once you start the task, it might seem easier to continue it.

Dr. Barbara Oakley, pictured here, teaches an online course called "Learning How to Learn." This course teaches students how the brain learns, how to increase memory, and how to deal with procrastination. Dr. Oakley is also an **engineering** professor.

CHAPTER SEVEN

STAY FOCUSED

Once you start doing a task, try to keep going. Stick with it! Try to ignore distractions. This is one of the reasons it can be good to have your own workspace, especially if you can shut other people out. Then you can focus on your task instead of trying to see what's on the television or what sort of trouble your brothers or sisters might be getting into.

If you catch yourself getting distracted, try to think about how good it will feel to complete your task. Then you can have free time without worrying about it! It can be good to take little breaks to stretch or get a drink of water. However, after you've taken your break, try to get right back to work. Fight the distractions! You can do it.

Avoiding distractions can be hard, especially when you feel there are more interesting things to do.

CHAPTER EIGHT

FINISH IT

Once you've finished your task, whether it's practicing violin, doing a household chore, or completing a homework assignment, it can also be tempting to just rush on to the next task or off to do something fun. However, be sure to finish things up the right way. This can save you time and trouble later.

Your homework has to be done, but it also has to be neat and readable. You should also put it somewhere you'll remember.

Take one last look at your homework and put it in your backpack so you don't forget it. Make sure it's neat and in a folder or something that protects it. Make sure the things you used to do a chore, such as dish towels or cleaning supplies, are neatly put away. Put your violin in its case so it's protected and you don't have to worry about it later. You'll be glad you did.

CHAPTER NINE

ORGANIZING TOOLS

Assignment notebooks and lists can be good organizing tools, but there are other tools you can use. Folders and notebooks for each subject can help keep your schoolwork organized. You could even use a different color for each subject so it's easy to tell which one is which. Take papers out of your school bag as soon as they're no longer needed and ask your parents if they can help you find a good place to keep them at home.

It can also be a good thing to get all your clothes, lunch, and school supplies ready the night before. That way, you don't have to rush around and find them in the morning. You can just grab them and go.

Sometimes families can work together to create and use organizing tools. You can create a family calendar and list everyone's **schedule** on it.

A family calendar can be very useful. That way, each family member can see what, when, and where things are going on.

Mom

TO DO LIST — TO DO — DONE

TO DO LIST	TO DO	DONE
Yoga	✓	
Pick up clothes	✓	
Package the lunches	✓	
Laundry		✓
Practice drawing	✓	
Cook favorite treat	✓	
Read 30 minutes		✓
Time for hobby	✓	
Wash the dishes	✓	
Gym		✓
Farmer's Market		✓
Cleaning	✓	

Dad

TO DO LIST	TO DO	DONE
Run for 30 minutes	✓	
Drive kids to school	✓	
Lawn		✓
Special Projects		✓
Take the garbage out	✓	
Go to the zoo with kids	✓	
Take a trip with family	✓	
Walk /feed dog	✓	
Time for hobby		✓
Car service		✓
Golf	✓	
Boss BBQ		✓

Mia

TO DO LIST	TO DO	DONE
Practice the violin	✓	
Clean your room	✓	
Pick up clothes	✓	
Read 30 minutes		✓
Homework	✓	
TV-time (30 min)	✓	
Walk the dog	✓	
Swimming		✓
Ballet	✓	

Good luck!

Luck!

Sunday	Monday	Tuesday	Wednesday	Thursday	Friday	Saturday
			Dentist 1	2	3	4
5	6 Yoga	7	Wash car 8	9	10 Swimming	11
12 bank	13	14 Shopping	15	Golf 16	17	18
19	20	21 Happy Birthday!	22	23	24	25 Pay bills
26 Post letter	27	28	29 Swimming	30	31 Car service	

Happy day.

Have a nice day!

Happy journey!

CHAPTER TEN

USE YOUR SKILLS!

Once you start getting more organized, you might find that you're more independent. Your parents might not have to bother or nag you to get things done as much. You might not have to ask for help as much, and they'll be able to trust you more! This can be a really good feeling. Organizational skills can help you throughout school and into adulthood. They're very useful.

Think of other ways to get organized. Maybe you can come up with a new organizational system for your room, so you always know where all of your things are. Maybe you can help arrange a new family **routine** that works better for everyone. Maybe you can help your friends get organized. If all of you have more time, you'll be able to do more fun things together!

GLOSSARY

assignment (uh-SYNE-muhnt) A task or amount of work given to do.

chore (CHOHR) A task.

distraction (duh-STRAK-shuhn) Something that takes attention away from something else.

engineering (en-juh-NEER-ing) The application of science to the goal of creating useful machines or structures.

equipment (uh-KWIHP-muhnt) Supplies or tools needed for a certain purpose.

extracurricular (ehk-struh-kuh-RIH-kyuh-luhr) Relating to activities that are offered by a school but are not part of the course of study.

fiercely (FEERS-lee) To a high degree.

focus (FOH-kuhs) To direct attention at something.

information (in-fuhr-MAY-shuhn) Knowledge or facts about something.

overwhelm (oh-vuhr-WEHLM) To overpower in thought or feeling.

priority (pry-OHR-uh-tee) Something that's considered more important than other things.

routine (roo-TEEN) A regular way of doing things in a particular order.

schedule (SKEH-jool) A list of times when certain events will happen.

INDEX

PRIMARY SOURCE LIST

Page 9
Richard Branson in Genoa, Italy. Photograph. July 20, 2018. Vincenzo Lombardo.

Page 11
The Obama family, including, from left, Michelle, Sasha, Malia, and Barack Obama, on the White House lawn. Photograph. April 14, 2009. Charles Ommanney.

Page 15
Dr. Barbara Oakley backstage during the annual Headmasters' and Headmistresses' Conference (HMC) at the Europa Hotel in Belfast, Ireland. Photograph. October 2, 2017. Niall Carson.

WEBSITES

Due to the changing nature of Internet links, PowerKids Press has developed an online list of websites related to the subject of this book. This site is updated regularly. Please use this link to access the list: www.powerkidslinks.com/SSEL/incharge